SOMEBODY'S HERO

Melissa Lautigar

Balboa Press books may be ordered through booksellers or by contacting:

Balboa Press
A Division of Hay House
1663 Liberty Drive
Bloomington, IN 47403
www.balboapress.com
844-682-1282

ISBN: 978-1-9822-5748-4 (sc)
ISBN: 978-1-9822-5749-1 (e)

Library of Congress Control Number: 2020921334

Print information available on the last page.

Balboa Press rev. date: 11/11/2020

BALBOA.PRESS
A DIVISION OF HAY HOUSE

SOMEBODY'S HERO

To my 4th grade students who inspire me every day.

I was a hero to somebody.

Never mind how big or small.

I was a hero to somebody,

to some people at the mall.

The door was opened for a family whose young ones wailed and cried.

Also, for an older guy who smiled as he walked by.

Just before the door was closed another man arrived.

Somebody in a wheelchair with a thankful high five.

I was a hero to somebody.

I didn't need to talk.

I was a hero to somebody,

To a man on the sidewalk.

This man didn't have a lot of things, but a sad look on his face.

There was cardboard and some other things that cluttered up his space.

I felt strange walking by him, and I didn't know what to say,

so I smiled, waved, and said to him, "Have a very nice rest of your day!"

I was a hero to somebody.

I am sure it is a thing.

I was a hero to a robin, who was tied up in some string.

My walk took me past him, as he was trying to take flight.

I had to run to catch him before I could untie.

After he was relieved of the string around his neck,

he flew so fast away from me and landed on a deck.

I was a hero to somebody.

This was really cool.

I was a hero to somebody, to a student at my school.

There was a younger student, crying in the hall.

He didn't know what bus to take and didn't know who to call.

I took him to a teacher, who had a big, long list.

She helped him find his bus, before it was ever missed.

I was a hero to somebody.

I didn't mean to make a fuss.

I was a hero to somebody,

To a girl who rides my bus.

There was a group of kids, who were not very nice.

They would be called bullies if that title was suffice.

These kids had been throwing things at some undeserving girl.

It was really bad that day, when they went on a name calling whirl.

I don't know what got into me, but I'd really had enough.

I stood up and yelled some things to make them all shut up.

They sat down and turned around, which was extremely strange.

Sometimes you have to stand up to bullies, if you want to see some change.

I was a hero to somebody.

I wasn't messing around.

I was a hero to somebody,

Up on the school playground.

I thought it was important to let the younger kids join in.

They love to play with us every day, no matter if they win.

Soccer, hockey, and football are our favorite games to play.

We cheer and yell and shout hooray when they get a break away.

I was a hero to somebody.

Each and every fall.

I was a hero to my neighbor,

and I always have a "ball."

This man does not get out much, he has a cane to walk.

I see him every now and then, and he really likes to talk.

I rake his leaves and bag them, but jump in them as well.

He watches from the window smiling, I can always tell.

I was a hero to somebody.

Something I couldn't see.

I was a hero to somebody,

A cat up in a tree.

I heard a faint meow, trotting home from school.

I looked all around me, and saw the cat up there, but how?

The neighbor said her dog had chased the cat away.

Up in the tree to take cover, it went up there to stay.

The cat heard me calling, so she started her way down.

I ran up and grabbed the cat, before she hit the ground.

I was a hero to somebody,

This time from the heart.

I was a hero to somebody,

Before the hockey game could start.

The school was collecting donations, for a kid who was badly hurt.

I felt sad, because I knew him, he played hockey with the squirts.

With five dollars from the tooth fairy, I knew exactly what to do.

That family needed it more than me, so I made a donation too.

I was a hero to somebody.

Fulfilling someone's dream.

I was a hero to somebody,

To a member on my team.

Playing hockey is my passion, skating up and down the ice.

I score goals all the time, which is really kind of nice.

This game was a little different, because the game was on the line.

It was a lot of fun that day, because it was my teammates' turn to shine.

I got the puck from Cal, who passed it up to Jake.

He was waiting to receive it, and he knew what was at stake.

The clock ticked down to zero as he shot it at the net.

His first goal of the season, the one he'll never forget.

I was a hero to somebody.

This time I was really glad.

I was a hero to somebody,

To my one and only dad.

We had a gigantic snowstorm, and it wasn't going to stop.

I think there was a snowfall record, we were surely at the top.

My dad had to work all night and then came home to plow.

I felt really bad for him, looking back at it now.

To his surprise the job was done. The shovel in the bank.

It was the one and only me that he would have to thank.

I was a hero to somebody.

This time it was we.

We were heroes to somebody,

To those we never see.

We pooled our Christmas money, to help some kids in need.

These kids are sick with cancer, who needed cheering up indeed.

Our class made tie fleece blankets to provide the kids a snuggle.

While staying in the hospital supporting their big struggle.

See, kids don't need everything for Christmas, especially from a store.

Sometimes, if we work together, we can achieve so much more.

I was a hero to somebody.

Someone important to me.

I was a hero to somebody,

It was my mom don't you see?

She works so hard to support me,

through everything under the sun.

I wanted to help her out a bit, so she could have some fun.

I dusted, vacuumed, and picked up the very best I could.

I hope she liked the cookies I made. I knew she really would.

I was a hero to somebody.

Definitely more than one.

I was a hero to somebody,

During a pandemic that wasn't fun.

Doing things for people to lighten up the mood.

It was just a little thing, but it was on a large, scale magnitude.

Bracelets for the frontline workers, who were out there saving lives.

To fifty states and Canada in hopes that they would thrive.

You don't have to do big things to be a hero, I say.

Sometimes it is the little things you do

each and every day.

Take some time to think about,

the nice things that you do.

Be proud that the hero in this story,

Really might be you!

Take a moment to write your own hero moment.

Printed in the United States
By Bookmasters